SOM
DIALECT

A selection of words and anecdotes
from around Somerset

by
Louise Maskill

BRADWELL
BOOKS

Published by Bradwell Books
9 Orgreave Close Sheffield S13 9NP
Email: books@bradwellbooks.co.uk

© Louise Maskill 2014

All rights reserved. No part of this publication may be
reproduced, stored in a retrieval system or transmitted
in any form or by any means, electronic, mechanical,
photocopying, recording or otherwise without the prior
permission of Bradwell Books.

British Library Cataloguing in Publication Data:
a catalogue record for this book is available from
the British Library.

1st Edition

ISBN: 9781902674896

Print: Gomer Press, Llandysul, Ceredigion SA44 4JL

Artwork and design by: Andrew Caffrey

Photograph Credits:
Unless otherwise stated, all images supplied by
old-photos.co.uk. Old-photos.co.uk have supplied images
derived from old postcards or old photographs and to the
best of their knowledge the images are out of copyright.
Any claims to ownership of copyright should be addressed
to old-photos.co.uk
Glastonbury Tor, the Church of St. John the Baptist
© Andrew and Susan Caffrey

SOMERSET DIALECT

by Louise Maskill

ACKNOWLEDGEMENTS

This book came together at the request and with the support of Chris Gilbert; I am indebted to him for research materials, guidance and for his faith in me. Tom, Molly, Owen and Caitlin have encouraged and supported me throughout and made their own contributions to the A-to-Z, and have put up with me practising my Somerset accent as I discovered many of the words in this book. Tom also read drafts and sourced pictures, finding errors aplenty in early versions of the manuscript. Any that remain are my responsibility, not his.

As always, huge thanks to all of you.

DEDICATION

For **TOM**

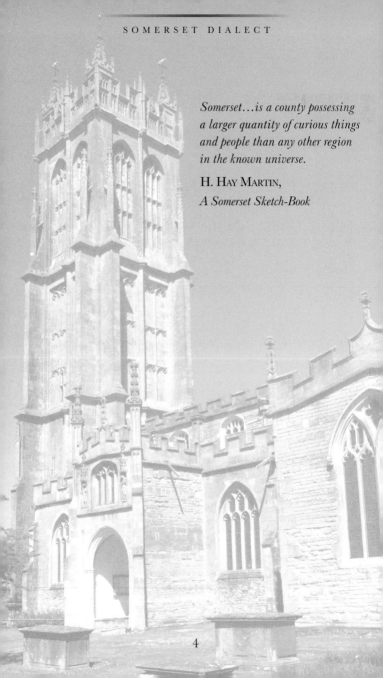

*Somerset…is a county possessing
a larger quantity of curious things
and people than any other region
in the known universe.*

H. HAY MARTIN,
A Somerset Sketch-Book

Introduction

Although dialects are still evident in everyday speech from different parts of the country, they are nowhere near as common or as diverse as they used to be. This gradual extinction has been noted and mourned by writers and antiquarians over many years, and huge efforts have been made to capture the colloquial speech of men and women from various parts of the country.

Somerset is an ancient and mystical part of the British Isles, and the research for this book has taken me on a journey down winding country lanes, in and out of apple orchards, into caves, up and down hills and even to the Holy Land. The pure dialect of this part of Britain is as close as any modern speech to the language of our Anglo-Saxon forbears, and as such it triggers moments of almost-recognition as rediscovered ancient words are echoed in modern pronunciation and usage.

The first part of this book is an A to Z of words and phrases arranged with their meanings and a few examples of usage, while the second part contains a collection of anecdotes, stories, rhymes and curiosities, all arranged by theme. Some of the words in the A to Z are now in common use in everyday English, but the aim is to indicate their provenance in the old Somerset dialect. The anecdotes may be long or short, complicated or simple, but all contain genuine examples of Somerset dialect as gathered by myself or recorded by historians and collectors over the years.

I hope this book might contribute in some small way to preserving a few of the words which were once in common use but which now face extinction.

Louise Maskill

Allerford pack horse bridge
Shutterstock ©Tony Brindley

A

A – yes, or he

Aa'th – earth

Abbey – the white poplar tree

Abbey-lubber – a lazy idle fellow

Abrood – descriptive of a hen who is sitting on a clutch of eggs

Acker – friend

Afeared – afraid, frightened

After – alongside

Afore, aforn or avaur – before

Agallied – frightened, scared

Agin – against

Agon – gone by

Aine – to throw stones at

Aller – the alder tree

Allonce – all of us, everyone

Amawst – almost, nearly

Amper – a boil or pimple

An – if

Anby – some time from now, a short time later

Aneen – on end, upright

Angle – a fish-hook

Angle-dog or angle-twitch – an earthworm

Anty – empty

Apple drames – wasps that frequent orchards at harvest time

Apse – the aspen tree

Arg, argufy – to argue, hold an argument

Ascride – across or athwart

Aslun or aslew – diagonal or sloping

Astroddle – astride

Assue or asew – descriptive of a cow whose milk has been allowed to dry up in preparation for calving

Ater – after

Athin – within

Athout – without

Auverlook – to bewitch

Avraur – frozen, stiff with frost

Ax – to ask; or to waddle

Axen – ashes

Ayir – air

The village of Wheddon Cross, 1911

B

Backsunded – facing northwards

Backy – tobacco

Bade – bed

Ball – bald

Ballirag – to scold or verbally abuse

Balrib – a spare rib

Bane – a mortal disease, especially applied to sheep

Bannut – a walnut

Barrener – a cow not in calf

Bastick – a basket

Batch – a hillock or small hill

Bawker or bawker stone – a sharpening stone for metal implements such as scythes

Bease – cattle, oxen

Becall – to censure or rebuke, particularly a child

Bedfly – a flea

Bee-but or bee-lippen – a beehive

Beedy or biddy – a chick

Begorz or begummers – oaths often thrown into conversation
   Begorz, I ont tell.

Begrumpled – offended, upset

Belg – to cry or shout aloud

Belk or bulk – to belch

Bell-flower or bell-rose – a daffodil

Benge – to drink to excess

Bennet – coarse long grass. Hence a field may be *bennetty*

Berrin – a funeral procession

Bethink – to grudge someone something

Betwattled – in a distressed and confused state of mind

Betwit – to rake up old grievances

Bibble – to drink often

Billid – mad, distracted or confused

Bim-boms – anything hanging, such as icicles, bells, or tassels on clothing

Binnick – the stickleback

Bivver – to quiver, tremble or shake

Blake – to faint

Blanker – a spark of fire

Blanscue – a misfortune or unexpected accident

Bleachy – descriptive of brackish water

Blunt – a storm of snow or rain

Bobbish – healthy, in good spirits

Boming – hanging down, like long hair on a woman

Boneshave – rheumatism

Booat – boat

Bow – an arched bridge

Bowerly – descriptive of a tall, well-built person

Brave – in good health, or recovering after sickness

Brazed – cramped and stiff with cold

Brickle or brickly – fragile, easily broken

Brimmle or brummel – a bramble

Brit – to indent or make an impression on a solid surface

Brock – a piece of peat dried for fuel

Bruckle or bruckly – applied to objects: muddled, incoherent
   My things are in a bruckle state.

Bucked – having a strong goaty taste (applied to cheese)

Buckle – a dispute or quarrel

Bumtowel – a long-tailed tit

Bungee – anything that is short, wide and squat in shape

Buss – a half-grown calf

Butty – a partner

Buzzies – flies or other miscellaneous buzzing insects

Bwile – to boil

Bwye – goodbye, farewell

The old walnut trees in Carhampton village, 1903

C

Cag – to irritate, annoy or vex

Callyvan – a pyramidal trap for catching birds

Cas – because

Cass'n or cassn't – cannot

Caterpillar – the cockchafer

Chackle – to make a noise like a hen

Chaity – careful, pleasant, neat

Cham – to chew

Chayer – a chair

Chick-a-beedy – a chick

Chilbladder – a chilblain

Chilver – a ewe-lamb

Chimley – a chimney

Chissom – to bud or put out shoots

Choor – any kind of dirty household work. Hence *choory*, to do housework

Chuggy pig – a woodlouse

Chump – a log for the fire

Clammer – a footpath up a steep bank

Clamper – a difficulty or problem

Clathers – clothes or rags

Clavy or clavypiece – a mantelpiece

Clear and sheer, or cliver and shiver – completely, utterly

Clim – to climb

Clinkers – hoof marks

Clinker-bell – an icicle

Coase – coarse, rough

Cob-wall – a wall made of clay mixed with straw

Cockygee, cockagee – a small sour apple

College – a short row of tenement houses with only one entrance from the street

Colley – a blackbird

Collop – salted meat

Comical – odd, curious or remarkable

Conk or skonk – a collection of people

Cop-bone – the kneecap

Count – to think or believe

Coupie, croupie – to crouch, as in *coupie down*

Cow-baby – a coward or timid person

Crap – a sudden sharp sound, a snap or a crack

Creem – a sudden fit of shivering

Crewel – the cowslip

Creeze – squeamish or dainty

Crips – crisp

Crowdy or crowdy-kit – a violin. Hence *crowder,* a violinist or fiddler

Crowner – coroner. Hence *to be crowned* was to have an inquest held over a dead body by the coroner

Crowst – crust. Hence *crowsty* – snappish, surly

Crub or crubbin – food, particularly bread and cheese

Cruel – intensive, very much, as in cruel-kind, extremely kind

Cute – sharp or clever

Cutty – small, diminutive; or a wren

D

Dade – dead

Daddick – rotten wood. Hence daddicky, rotten or perished; sometimes applied also to the old and feeble

Daddy granfer – a woodlouse

Daggers – a type of sedge grass with sharp serrated leaves

Dandy – distracted

Dap – to hop or bounce, like a ball; or the habits and peculiarities of a person

I know all the daps on'm.

Dave – to thaw

Daver – to fall down, fade or droop

Dewberry – a kind of blackberry

Dew-bit – an early snack taken before breakfast

Dibs – money

Diddlecome – angry, sorely vexed or distracted

Digence – a word for the Devil

Dilly – cranky or odd

Dird – thread

Dirsh or drush – a thrush

Dirt – earth generally, as in a garden. Hence *dirten* – made of earth

Don – to put on. Hence *donnins* – clothes

Doughboy – a dumpling

Dout – to put out or extinguish

Down-daggered – disconsolate or melancholy

Dowst – dust; or money

  Come, down wi' tha dowst! (Come on, put your money down!)

Drang – a narrow path or lane

Drapper – a small tub

Drauve – a drove, or road leading to fields or pasture

Drean – to drawl or drone in speaking or reading

Dreckley – soon, sometime, never. Similar to mañana

Dreaten – to threaten

Drimmeling – slow, continuous, dragging pain

Dring – to throng or press, as in a crowd

Dringet – a crowd or throng

Droa – to throw

Drode – threw or thrown

Drool – to drivel or talk nonsense

Drow or drowy – to dry

  The hay do drowy ter'ble now.

Drub – to throb

Druck – to cram down or press into a receptacle

Dub or dubby – blunt, squat

Dudder – to deafen with loud noise; to become confused

and overloaded with sound

Duds – dirty clothes

Dumbledore – a honeybee, or else a stupid fellow

Dumpsey or dimpsey – twilight, the half-light at the end of the day

It were the dumps of the yavening.

Dunch – deaf

Durns – a door frame

Dunster village, 1906

E

Eake – also, as well

Ear-keckers – the tonsils

Eese – yes

Eet – yet

Elmen – made out of or belonging to the elm tree

Emmers – embers

Emmets – ants. Hence *emmet-batch* – an ant hill. Alternatively, a derogatory term for a tourist

En – him

    A zid en. (He saw him.)

Errish or herrish – stubble in the fields

Et – that

Eve – to become damp by absorbing moisture from the air

Evet – a lizard or newt

Ex – an axle

Eye – the space beneath the arch of a bridge

F

Fags! – an exclamation: Really? Indeed!

Fairy or fare – a weasel

Fauth or foth – the turning place of a plough at the edge of a field

Fell – to sew down a hem

Fend – to forbid

Fess – smart

Fester – an inflammation, boil or tumour

Fig – a raisin. Hence *figged pudding* – a pudding with raisins in it

Filtry – filth, dirt, rubbish

Firnd – friend

Fitch or fitchet – a polecat

A was as cross as a fitchet.

Fitten or vitten – an idle fancy or whim

Fleet – to float

Flittermouse – a bat

Flush – (of young birds) fledged, able to fly

Foggy – fat, corpulent

Footer – a term of contempt for unsavoury folk

Footy – insignificant, of no consequence

Forrel – the cover of a book

Forweend – (of young children) peevish or difficult to please

French-nut – the walnut

Fur – to throw

Furcum – the bottom of something; the whole thing

Fuz or fuzzen – the gorse bush

When fuz is out o' blossom,
Kissing's out o' fashion.

Fuz-pig – a hedgehog

G

Gaern – a garden

Gain – handy, adept at something

Gale – an old castrated bull

Gallibagger – a bugbear or bogeyman

Gally – to frighten or scare. Hence *gallid* – frightened

Ganny-cock – a turkeycock

Gare – the ironwork for wheels, waggons and so on

Gaffer – an old man

Gamble – a leg

Gawcum – a simpleton

Gib or gibby – a pet lamb

Giffin – a triflingly small portion of time

Gifts – the white spots in fingernails

Giggletin – (of females) wanton or trifling

Gimmace – a hinge

Ginnin – beginning

Girnin – grinning

Girt – great

Gird'l – a great deal

Glare – the glaze on earthenware; or to apply glaze to an unfired pot

Gleanie – a guinea fowl

Glou-beason – a glow-worm

Glutch – to swallow

Gollop – a large morsel

Goose-cap – a silly person

Gout – a drain or gutter

Gribble – a young apple tree raised from seed

Grig – to pinch

Gripe – a small drain or ditch

Grockle – a derogatory term for a tourist or visitor. Hence *grockle-shell*, a caravan or touring motor home

Gruff – a mine or mineworking. Hence *gruffer* – a miner

Guddle – to drink fast and greedily. Hence a *guddler* – a greedy drinker

Gulch – a sudden swallow or gulp

Gumpy – lumpy or bumpy

Gush – to increase blood flow by giving someone a fright
   A' gied I sich a gush.

Gwon – gone

The main street, Kilve, 1908

H

Hack or hacket – to hop on one leg, or to play a game of hopscotch or similar

Hacker – to stammer or chatter with cold

Hain – to keep cattle out of a field so that it can be mowed

Haling – coughing

Hallantide – All Saints' Day, the 1st November

Halse – the hazel tree

Halve or helve – to turn upside down

Ham – a rich flat pasture, usually near a river

Hange – offal from a pig or sheep

Hank – to have dealings with

Happer – to crackle or rattle, like hail on a roof

Hard – full-grown. Hence *hard people* – adults

Hark – listen. Often used sarcastically, as in *hark at 'ee!*

Harm – any contagious disease for which the specific name is not known

Hay-maidens – ground-ivy

Hearam-skearam – wild, or romantic

Heel – to hide or cover. Hence *heeler* – one who hides something

    Proverb: *The heeler is as bad as the stealer.*

Hell – to pour

Hellier – someone who lays the tiles on a roof

Helm – straw prepared for thatching

Hen – to throw

Hereright – directly, or in this place

Herret – a pitiful wretch

Hick – to hop on one leg

Hike – to go away or remove oneself

Hippety-hoppety – in a limping or hobbling manner

Hire – to hear or to be told

Hirn or hurn – to run

Hobblers – men employed to tow vessels (such as barges) with ropes

Hodmedod – short and squat

Hoke or hoak – to gore or wound with horns, like an ox

Holders – the canine teeth of a dog

Holm – the holly tree. Hence *holmen* – made of holly wood

Holme-screech – the missel thrush, from its habit of eating holly berries

Hoop – the bullfinch

Hoppet – to hop

Hornen – made of horn

Horse-godmother – a masculine woman

Horse-stinger – the dragonfly

Houzen – houses

How – to long for something

Hud – the skin or husk of a fruit or berry

Hug – the itch

Hulder – to hide or conceal

Hully – a long wicker trap used for catching eels

Hulve – to turn over or up-end

Humdrum – a small three-wheeled cart drawn by one horse

I

I – yes

Idleton – an idle fellow

Inin – an onion

Insense – to inform

Ire – iron

Ist – east. Hence *istard* – eastward

It – yet

J

Jack-in-the-lantern or Joan-in-the-wad – a will o' the wisp

Jib – a wooden stand for a barrel

Jitch or jitchy – such

Jod – the letter J

Jonick – fair or straightforward

Jorum – a large jug or bowl full of something to eat or drink

Jot – to knock while writing, causing blots or smudges

The village of Cheddar, 1903

K

Kecker – the windpipe or trachea

Keep – a large basket

Keeve or kive – a large vessel or tub used in brewing

Keffel – a bad or worn-out horse

Kerning – the process of turning from blossom to fruit

Kill – a kiln

Kilter – money

Kircher – the midriff or stomach area

Kirsmas – Christmas

Kirsen – to christen a child

Kit – a tribe or gang

Knap – a small hill or rise in the ground

Knottlins – the intestines of a pig prepared for food

Knot-sheep – a sheep without horns

L

Labber – to loll the tongue out of the mouth, as does a dog

Lade-pail – a small pail with a long handle, used for filling bigger vessels

Lady Buddick – a type of early apple

Lady-cow – a ladybird

Laiter – the collection of eggs laid by a hen

She have laid out her laiter.

Lamager – lame or crippled

Larks' leers – arable land not currently in use; a favoured habitat for larks

Lart or lawt – a loft

Lary or leary – empty, thin

Lay-field – a field laid down to grass

Leat – to leak, or a place where water leaks out

Learn or larn – to teach

Who larned 'e thay tricks?

Leathern-mouse or leathern-bird – the bat

Leer – empty

Lent – to loan, or the use of anything borrowed

Lew – sheltered from storms or wind

Libbets – tatters or little bits

Lidden – a story or song

Liggen or ligget – a rag

Lights – the lungs

Lighting stock – a mounting block, for getting onto or off a horse

Linny – an open shed attached to a barn or outhouse

Lip or lippen – a generic term for something that contains something else. Hence a *bee-lippen*, a beehive, or a *seed-lip*, a seed container

Lipary – wet and rainy

Lirrop – to beat or thrash

Lob – to hang down or droop

Lock – a small quantity, as in a lock of hay or a lock of straw

Lock-a-daisy! – exclamation of surprise or pleasure

Longful – taking a long time

Lumper – to move heavily, trudge or stumble

Lurden – a sluggard or lazy person

Luvver – friend, mate

Alright, my luvver?

M

Mace – acorns

Macky-moon – a man who plays the fool

Make-wise – to pretend

Mander – sort or kind, as in *all mander of things*

Mang – to mix together

Market-fresh – slightly tipsy, like a farmer on his way home from market after a good day's trading and socialising

Math – a litter of pigs

Maules – measles

Mawkin – a wetted cloth attached to a pole, used to clean out bakers' ovens

Mawn – a basket

Mazy – mad. Hence *mazy-house* – the madhouse
  She be a mazy ould vool.

Meech – to play truant from school

Mesh – moss, especially that which grows on oak trees

Mess or messy – to feed cattle with hay

Mig – mead. Often heard in the expression *as sweet as mig*

Milt – the spleen

Mind – to remember

Misky – misty, foggy

Mixen – a dunghill

Mizmaze – confusion, amazement

Mommacks – small pieces, fragments

Mommet or mommick – a scarecrow

Mooch – to stroke gently

Moot – to root up or dig out

Mop – a tuft of grass

More – the root of a tree

Mouse-snap – a mousetrap

Muddy-want – a mole

Mumper – a beggar

Marton main street, 1906

N

Nacker – a nag

Nant – aunt

Nap – a small hillock

Nawl – the naval

Neel, nill or neeld – a needle

N'eet – not yet

Nestle-tripe – the weakest and smallest bird in the nest.

May also be applied to be the smallest or weakest child in a family

Never the near – to no purpose

Nickle – to move along hastily but in an awkward manner

Niddick – the nape of the neck

Ninny-watch – a longing desire

Nist – nearby, near

Nitch – a burden

Nonation – difficult to understand; incoherent or wild

Noration – clamour, noise

Northern or northering – incoherent or foolish

Nosset – a plain and simple dish, such as might be suitable for a sick person

Not-sheep – a sheep without horns

Not or knot – a flowerbed

Nug – an unshaped piece of timber

Nummet – a small meal between breakfast and dinner

Nuncle – uncle; or to cheat someone

Nuther – neither

O

Oddments – odd things, or offal

Office – the eaves of a house

Onlight – to get off a horse

Orchit – an orchard

Ordain – to intend something

Ornd – fated, pre-ordained

Orra-one – anyone, everyone

Orseny or oseny – to forbode or predict

Ort – art

Oten – often

Ourn – ours

Overget – to overtake

Overlook – to bewitch or charm

Over-right – opposite, facing

P

Pack-an-penny day – the last day of a fair, when bargains are sold off

Pair of stairs – a staircase with two landings

Panchard night – Shrove Tuesday

Pank – to pant, breathe heavily

Parfit – perfect

Parget – to plaster the inside of a chimney with lime mortar

Parrick – a paddock

Payze – to raise up with a lever

Peel – a pillow or bolster

Pennin – a temporary enclosure for feeding and watering animals

Pick – a two-pronged pitchfork for making hay

Pigs-looze – a pigsty

Pilch, pilcher – a baby's nappy

Pilm or pilllum – fine dust which floats in the air

Pind or pindy – fusty, as of corn or flour which has started to go mouldy

Pinions – the refuse wool after combing

Pink-twink – a chaffinch

Pitch – to lay unshaped stones together to make a road; or to lay on the ground, as of snow

Pit-hole – a grave

Pix, pex or pixy – to pick up apples in an orchard after the main crop has been harvested

Plim – to swell or increase in size

Plud – the muddy surface of a freshly ploughed wet field

Poached – broken up, raised, as of a muddy and rough field
   The ground's poaching up, we'll a' ter bring the cattle in.

Pockfredden – marked on the face with smallpox scars

Pog – to thrust or push with the fist

Pomice, pomace, pummy or pummy-squat – apples crushed and pounded for making cider

Ponted – bruised and indented. Applied to apples on the edge of decay

Pook – the stomach

Porr – to stuff or cram with food

Pote – to push something through a small hole or confined space. Hence *poty* – confined, cramped

Power – a great deal of something

That was a power of rain.

Pray – to drive loose cattle into a single herd

Proud-tailor – the goldfinch

Pud – the hand or fist

Pulk or pulker – a small shallow place containing water

Pur – a male lamb

Puskey – short of breath, wheezing

Put – a small two-wheeled cart used on farms

Puxie – a place which is treacherous and marshy underfoot; commonly applied to places where springs rise to the surface

Pyer – a wooden guide rail along a bridge

Wraxall village cross, 1908

Q

Quar – to raise stones from a quarry. Hence *quar-man* – a quarry worker

Quare – queer, odd

Quarrel or quarrey – a square of window glass

Quat – full, satisfied; or sitting flat, like a bird on its eggs

Quilled – withered, like dry grass

Quine – a corner

Quirk – to complain, groan or grunt

R

Raft-up – disturb from sleep

Rain-pie – the woodpecker

Rake up – to cover or bury

Rally – to scold

Rames – the dead stalks of crop plants such as potatoes, cucumbers etc.

Rammel – descriptive of cheese made with unskimmed milk

Rampsing – tall

Ramshackle – loose or disjointed

Rampin – outrageously, extravagantly

Randy or randin – a riotous party or merry-making

Range – a sieve

Rangle – to twine or grow in a sinuous manner, like plants such as ivy or hops

Rap – to exchange

Rasty – rancid, or gross and obscene

Ratch – to stretch

Rathe-ripe – a type of early apple; or descriptive of fruit or people who mature early

Rawn – to devour greedily

Rawny – thin or meagre

Reballing – catching eels with earthworms attached to a ball of lead hung from a string

Reen – a water-course or open drain

Rere-mouse – a bat

Rexen – rushes

Rip – a vulgar old woman; or to chide, berate

Robin-riddick or robin-ruddock – a robin redbreast

Rode – to go out in the late evening or early morning to shoot wildfowl as they pass overhead

Roe-briar – the large dog-rose

Room or rhume – dandruff

Rose – of seeds, to drop out of the pod when overripe

Rout – to snore

Rozzim – a quaint saying or proverb

Ruck – to crouch down

Rudderish – hasty or without due care

Porlock village
thatcher, 1935

S

Sand-tot – a sandhill or dune

Sar or sarve – to earn wages

Sarrant – a servant

Scad – a short shower of rain

Scag – to tear or catch, like fabric on a nail

Scamblin – a small meal taken at irregular times

Scollop – an indentation or scooped notch

Scoose wi' – to talk with

Scorse or squiss – to exchange or barter

Scottle – to cut into pieces in a wasteful manner

Scrambed – numb with cold

Scrawf – waste, refuse

Screed – a shred

Scrint – to scorch

Scud – a scab

Scurrick – a small coin, the smallest denomination imaginable

  I haven't a scurrick to my name.

Sea-bottle – a particular type of seaweed with round or oval pods or bladders in the stalks

Sea-crow – a cormorant

Seam – a horse-load

Seltimes – seldom, not often

Seven-sleeper – the dormouse

Shab – the itch or the pox. May be cured by *shab-water,* a concoction of water, tobacco and mercury. Hence *shabby* – affected by the shab

Sharps – the shafts of a cart

Sheer – a sheath, e.g. for scissors or a knife

Shelving stone – blue tile or slate used for roofing houses

Shillith – a shilling's worth

Shod – to shed or spill

Showl – a shovel

Shride, shroud or shrig – to cut wood from the sides of growing trees

Shuckning – shuffling

Shug – to scratch or rub against

Shuttles or shittles – floodgates

Sig – urine

Skag – to catch with an accidental blow, or to wound slightly

Skeer-devil – the swift

Skeerings – hay made from pasture land

Skenter – an animal that will not fatten, no matter how well fed

Skiff-handed – left-handed, or awkward

Skiffling – whittling a stick

Skilly – oatmeal porridge

Skimmerton – two persons on one horse, seated back to back, are said to be riding skimmerton

Skram – to benumb with cold

Skrent – to burn or scorch

Skummer – grime or marks left by dirty liquid or soft dirt

Slait – a usual or accustomed path for sheep

Sleeze – applied to cloth, to come apart readily

Slen – slope

Slitter – to slide or skid

Slock – to obtain something by illegal or clandestine means, or to encourage others (particularly someone else's servants) to do so

Slommacking – untidy or slatternly

Slop – loose

Smash – a blow or fall by which something is broken

Snags – small sloe berries

Snake leaves – bracken, ferns

Snippy – mean or parsimonious

Snowl – the head

Sog – waterlogged ground

Sousen – ears

Sparkid – speckled

Spawl – a chip from a block of stone

Stickle – applied to hills, steep. Applied to water, rapidly flowing

Stomachy – obstinate, proud or haughty

Stout – a gnat or mosquito

Strad – a piece of leather tied around the leg to defend against thorns

Suant – descriptive of rows of peas or beans: straight, even

Sulsh – a spot or stain

Summer-voy – facial freckles caused by the sun

Swell or swill – to swallow

Sweetort – to court or woo

East Pennard village milk cart outside the church, c.1900

T

Tack – a shelf

Taffety – dainty or nice. Chiefly applied to food and eating habits

Tanbase – unruly behaviour

Tang – to tie

Tave – to throw the hands about wildly

Tawl-down – to stroke or smooth, as of a cat's back

Teap – a point or peak

Ted – to turn hay so that it dries evenly

Teery – faint, weak

Temptious – tempting, inviting

Theesam – these

Therence – from that place

Thic, thicky or thicky-there – that

Tho – then

I couldn't go tho, but I went later.

Tiff or tip – a small drink of alcoholic liquor

Tile – to put something in a place from which it might easily fall

Tilty – irritable, easily offended

Timmer – timber, wood. Hence *timmern*, made of wood

Timmersome – fearful, uneasy

Tine – to shut (e.g. a door), or else to enclose (e.g. sections of land)

Tite – to weigh

Titty-todger – a wren

Toke – to harvest apples

Toll – to entice, allure or encourage

Have a bit o' cheese to toll down th' bread.

Tossity – drunken

Touse – a blow on some part of the head

Tramp – a long walk or journey

Tranter – a carrier

Trig – sound, firm, neat, tidy

Trim – to beat

Truckle – to roll. Hence a *truckle bed*, a bed which rolls out from under another larger one

Tun – a chimney

Turmits or turnets – turnips

Tut – a hassock

Twick – to twist or jerk suddenly

Twily – restless or impatient

U

Under-creeping – sneaking, slinking

Unket – dreary, dismal, lonely

Up – to arise

Upping stock – a wooden or stone block for mounting horses

Upsides – on an equal or superior footing

Upsighted – a particular defect of vision which renders a person unable to look down

Utchy or itchy – used instead of the first person pronoun, I
What shall utchy do?

V

Vage or vaze – a voyage

Valch or vug – to thrust with the elbow or fist

Vang – to catch, receive or earn

Vare – a species of weasel

Vawth – a bank of earth prepared for manure

Mells village post office, 1905

Vay – to succeed or turn out well

It don't vay.

Vell – a membrane, particularly the stomach lining of a calf used in cheesemaking

Vent or vent-hole – a sleeve or button-hole in a shirt

Vier – fire

Vinned – mouldy or decayed

Vitty – properly, aptly

Vlear – a flea

Vlother – incoherent talk or nonsense

Vouce – strong, or sometimes nervous

W

Wammel or wamble – to wander to and fro in an irregular manner

Want or wont – a mole

Want-heave – a molehill

Ward – to wade

Wash-dish – the wagtail

Wassail – to drink success to the apple trees

Weepy – descriptive of an area with many springs

Well-apaid – appeased or satisfied

Well-at-ease – hearty and healthy

Wetshod – possessed of wet feet

Wevet – a spider's web

Whecker – to laugh in a vulgar or low manner

Whipswhile – a short time; the time between strokes of a whip

Whisbird – a term of reproach or reproof

Whister-twister – a sharp blow on the side of the head

Widver or widow-man – a widower

Willy – a general term for baskets of various sizes, often made from willow

Wine – wind

Witherguess – different

Witherwise – otherwise

Witt – fit

Wock or woek – the oak

Wont – a mole

Wood-quist – a woodpigeon

Wood-wall – a woodpecker

Wriggle – any narrow sinuous hole or tunnel

Wring – a press, as in a cider-wring

Wrizzled or wrizzley – shrivelled or wrinkled

X, Y, Z

Yacker – an acre

Yal – ale

Yalhouse – an alehouse

Yapern – an apron

Yappingale, yaffler or yuckle – a woodpecker

Yarm – arm

Yess – an earthworm

Yezy – easy

Yoak – the grease in wool. Hence *yoaky*, the greasy condition of wool straight off a sheep

Yokes – hiccups

Yourn – yours

Za – so

Zam – to heat for a long time without boiling

Zand – sand

Zatenfare – not overly blessed with intellect

Zenvy – wild mustard

Zitch – such

Zog – soft, soggy, marshy land

Zull – a plough

Zwail – to move about with the arms flapping up and down

Zwang – a swing

Zwodder – a drowsy state of body and mind

Batheaston village, 1906

Pronunciation and usage

As with East Anglia, the West Country dialects in popular culture are generally associated with farming and rural simplicity; generic *"Mummerzet"* as often heard in television and radio productions is often equated with foolishness, ignorance and a lack of education. The dialect is also associated with pirates, possibly in part because of the strong sea-faring and maritime tradition of the West Country but also due to various Hollywood representations of pirates, particularly those of Robert Newton in the 1950s. However, it is also true that Edward Teach, better known as Blackbeard, was a native of Bristol, so perhaps the modern *"ooh arr, me hearties"* brand of pirate-speak is not so far from the truth after all.

In fact, though, the ancient dialect of Somerset is a direct and valuable relic of the languages spoken by the Anglo-Saxons over a millennium ago and the native British Celts before them, and much can be learned from a study of the preservation of old forms of speech in the surviving dialect today. For example, the received modern pronunciation of wasp, *wosp*, is in fact a change from the original Anglo-Saxon *waps*, but a Somerset native might still refer to the pesky insects as *wapses*. Older forms are often echoed in the grammar, pronunciation and usage of the dialect, making its preservation and protection an imperative.

The dialect of Somerset is traditionally distinguished into two localised versions separated geographically by the River Parret. The river runs to the west of Yeovil, and is said to be the boundary to which Cenwealh, the Anglo-Saxon King of Wessex, drove the native Britons after a crushing defeat at the battle of Pen Hill near Wells in 656 AD. Both versions contain echoes of the old Anglo-Saxon tongue from which modern English evolved, but this heritage is particularly evident in the east and south of the county. West of the Parret the older Celtic influences can still be detected and the pronunciation is closer to that of Devon and Cornwall. Indeed, at one time, the differences between the two versions of the dialect were so marked that people from the east side of the county would have decided difficulty in understanding those from the west.

Anglo-Saxon influence can be heard in the sounding of Z for S, although this is not a general rule; words which elsewhere in the country begin with an S may sound in Zomerzet as if they begin with Z – like *zand*, *zeed* and *zyder*. It can also be found in the substitution of V for F and the addition of a lengthened R after vowel sounds at the end of words – so that flea becomes something like *vleear*, while fire becomes *vyer*. Other consonants are also substituted with other sounds, notably OO for W at the start of words, so that Walter becomes *Oolter*, and Wells becomes *Ools*. The hard sound of K or C is sometimes replaced by the softer QU, so that coat becomes *quoat* while corn becomes *quorn*.

One of the most remarkable features of the dialects of the west of England in general, and Somerset in particular, are the lengthened and exaggerated sounds given to the vowels A and E. The sound of A is open and long, as in father but somewhat lengthened; this applies to almost all words, even those that would normally have a shorter or more rounded vowel sound such as ball. The sound of E is somewhat akin to the French é, like the central vowel sound in pane or cane. Another peculiarity is that the sound of TH is commonly pronounced d, so that three becomes *dree* and through becomes *droo*. The vowel O is sometimes used instead of the A sound in words such as *lork* (lark) and *hort* (heart), and the order of consonant sounds is sometimes inverted within words so that brush may become *birsh* and clasp may become *claps*.

There is also a tendency to run words together to make composite words or phrases. One common example is the elision of the O sound in go in produce *g'in* (go in), *g'auf* (go off – you get the idea!), *g'on*, *g'up*, *g'under*, *g'auver* and so on. A common politeness is the utterance *cheerzen*, a contraction of cheers, then (thank you).

There are many oddities of usage in the West Country dialects, and one such in Somerset is the difference between pitching and paving. To *pitch* a road was to lay unshaped, irregular or rough stones together to form a road or path, such as one might find across a stretch of muddy moorland. However, *paving* was much more formal, with paved ways being smooth and laid with evenly-shaped stones neatly fitted together to make an even surface fit for wheeled vehicles.

Some ancient and formerly obsolete words from Somerset dialect have found their way into common usage, not least because of their adoption and use by popular authors. However, the meanings of words are often changed by this process; the best-known example of this is the word *dumbledore*, an old Somerset dialect name for the bumble bee which was used by J.K. Rowling as the name of a character in her Harry Potter novels. Indeed, Hagrid, another character in the books, speaks in a dialect which closely resembles Somerset and which has been faithfully created by the author to sound correct as it is read aloud.

The village of Washford, 1906

History, traditions and customs

Somerset has a rich history of settlement from the earliest times, with the fertile Somerset Levels in particular being rich in archaeological remains. The Romans occupied the area for nearly four centuries, and after they withdrew from the British Isles they were eventually succeeded by the Anglo-Saxons, although it took two hundred years for the Saxons to wrest Somerset from native British hands. Some of the most pivotal battles in English history took place in Somerset, with the Anglo-Saxon king Alfred the Great fleeing to the Somerset Levels following his defeat by the Danes after a surprise attack at Chippenham in Wiltshire. Alfred launched a series of guerrilla attacks on the Danish army from the marshes around Athelney, and many of the best-beloved tales about Alfred's reign took place during this period of flight and armed resistance in Somerset. In perhaps the most famous tale, while in hiding Alfred accepted hospitality from a peasant woman, the wife of a swineherd, who was ignorant of his identity. She asked the king to mind some cakes that were baking by the fire, but, distracted by his thoughts about the plight of his kingdom, he allowed the cakes to burn. Legend suggests that the peasant woman was not best pleased, berating the king for his idleness and complaining that he couldn't be bothered to turn the cakes although he was happy to eat them when they were cooked. Rather than standing on his rank, the king humbly accepted her chastisement and even helped her bake a second batch. He went on from this edifying experience to fortify the Isle of Athelney, from where he defeated the Danes at the battle of Eddington in 878, securing the Danelaw and the independence of his kingdom of Wessex.

The Somerset tradition of *wassailing*, or singing to the apple trees, dates back many centuries at least to pre-Roman pagan times and now takes place on 17th January (the old Twelfth Night, before the calendars changed from the Julian to the Gregorian version in the eighteenth century). The word wassail comes from the Anglo-Saxon *waes hael* – good health. Exact customs vary, but there are some common themes throughout the southwest of England – a wassail king and queen are often selected to lead a procession from one orchard to the next accompanied by music and song. The queen (or sometimes the youngest person present) is lifted up into the boughs of the trees where she deposits toast soaked in wassail, the hot mulled cider which is an integral part of the ceremony. Then there is much loud singing and dancing between and around the trees, intended to drive away evil spirits, awaken the trees from their winter slumber and ensure a good harvest the following autumn.

The traditional wassailing hymn is sung:

Here's to thee, old apple tree,
Bloom well, and blow well, and bear apples enow!
Hats full, caps full,
Bushel-bushel sacks full,
An' my pockets full too!
Hurrah! Hurrah!

With the final shouts of "*hurrah!*" there is a great crescendo of noise, with singing, shouting and banging of drums and pots; shotguns may be fired into the air, and in some places the trees are even struck or beaten with sticks to wake them up. Then the whole procession would move on to the next farm. It was firmly believed that if the custom of wassailing was neglected the next autumn's crop of apples would be poor, and if a farmer was unpopular his farm might be "accidentally" left out of the wassailing round.

There are other Somerset traditions associated with apples and apple trees; one states that if a tree bears fruit and blossom at the same time it is regarded as an exceedingly bad omen which foretells a death in the family before the next spring. If a young woman peels an apple in one long strand and then throws the skin over her shoulder, tradition states that the shape formed by the fallen strand will resemble the first letter of the name of her future husband (some versions of this tradition suggest that she must carry out the ritual and observe the apple peel by the light of a full moon).

Another old Somerset folk tale relates to the wassailing custom, telling of the Apple Tree Man who is the spirit of the most venerable apple tree in an orchard. In the story a farmer offers his last mug of mulled cider to his apple trees, and is rewarded by the Apple Tree Man who shows him the location of buried treasure. Whatever the utility of these customs, the fact remains that Somerset apples and the cider which is made from them are still a mainstay of the local economy, and they are rarely bettered. Perhaps all the accumulated centuries of wassailing are still paying off.

Cheddar Road, Shipham village, c.1900

Shrove Tuesday, the first day of Lent, has a number of associated customs. The day before Shrove Tuesday used to be known as Collop Monday – *collop* being a dialect term for salted meat, which often had to be eaten up before the start of Lent.

A tradition similar to trick-or-treat was *crocking*, which involved youngsters throwing dirt or broken crockery into houses and making off without being caught. The customary cry was *"Tippety tappetty toe, give me a pancake and then I'll go."* It is easy to see why this tradition has been discouraged into extinction.

One famous story told around the county was the tragic tale of Fanny Fear, retold and remembered in a popular ballad. The story was allegedly true, occurring somewhere near the village of Shapwick; Fanny was a comely and virtuous farm girl whose heart was won by a young farm labourer named John. However, John was poor and felt himself unable to marry the fair Fanny until he had a better-paid job. He sought more lucrative work for four years, during which period the young couple courted and laid plans for the future, and eventually he was offered a job as a huntsman with a local gentleman. Overjoyed, Fanny began to make plans for their wedding the following summer.

However, one bitter wintry night the hounds in John's charge began to bay and yell, and he rushed from his bed in his nightshirt to see what had upset them. The next morning his mangled body was found in the kennels; the hounds had turned on him and killed him. Poor Fanny was stricken with grief, fainting dead away when she was told of John's grisly fate, and when she regained consciousness she had quite lost her reason; the ballad reports that all she could say was, *"Why did he goo in the cawld ta shiver? – Niver, o Jan, sholl I see thee. Niver!"*

The story might have ended there, recorded for posterity in ballad form, but William Jennings prints a letter from one Teddy Band, a poor cottager who had heard the ballad and felt he needed to comment on its "morils". The letter read as follows, proving that not all countrymen were fans of bloodsports and the keeping of hounds.

I a red thic ballet called Fanny Fear, an, zim ta I, there's naw moril to it. Nif zaw be you da then zo well o't, I'll gee one.

I dwont want to frunt any ov the gennelmen o' tha country, bit I always a thawt it desperd odd, that dogs should be kept in a kannel, and kept a hungered too, zaw that tha mad be moor eager ta hunt thic poor little theng called a hare. I dwon naw, bit I da

thenk, nif I war a gennelman, that I'd vine better spoort than huntin; bezides, zim ta I 'tis desperd wicked ta hunt animals vor one's spoort. Now, jitch a horrid blanscue as what happened at Shapick, niver could a bin but vor tha hungry houns. I haup that gennelmen ool thenk o't oten; an when tha da hire tha yell o' tha houns tha'll not vorgit Fanny Fear; a-maybe tha mid be zummet tha wiser an better vor't; I'm shower jitch a story desarves ta be remimbered. This is the moril.

I am, zur, your sarvant, Teddy Band.

Esme, who lived in East Quantox around 1910

Of course, the most famous tale of Somerset folklore is the story of the Holy Thorn of Glastonbury, brought from the Holy Land by Joseph of Arimathea, a relative of Jesus and a secret disciple who claimed Jesus' body after the crucifixion and buried it in his own prepared tomb in the garden of his house.

The story goes that Joseph, a wealthy trader, came to Britain in the years after Jesus' death and founded the first Christian church in Glastonbury when his staff, which he laid down on the ground beside him while he slept on Wearyall Hill above the town, miraculously took root and grew into a thorn tree. A few precious examples of the Glastonbury Thorn, a particular variety of hawthorn which flowers twice a year and usually bears blossom at Christmas, still grow in the area and a flowering sprig is sent to the Queen every year. Glastonbury Tor is often identified with the Isle of Avalon, the mystical land where King Arthur is said to sleep awaiting his return to defend the British Isles in their time of greatest need; the legend of the Glastonbury Thorn is told over the page in dialect form:

A summer afternoon on the summit of Glastonbury Tor

Who hath not hird o' Avalon?
'Twar talked o' much and long agon.
Tha wonders o' tha Holy Thorn,
Tha'which, zoon ater Christ war born,
Here planted war by Arimathea,
This Joseph that com'd auver sea,
An planted Kirstianity.

Tha za that whun a landed vust
(Zich plazen war in God's own trust)
A stuck iz staff into tha groun
An auver iz shoulder lookin roun,
Whatever mid iz lot bevall,
A cried aloud, "Now, weary all!"
Tha staff het budded an het grew,
An at Kirsmas bloom'd the who da droo.
An still het blooms at Kirsmas bright,
But best tha za at dork midnight.
An pruf o' this, if pruf you will,
Iz voun in tha name o' Wearyall Hill!

A Glastonbury
Holy Thorn.

The Church of St. John the Baptist with Holy Thorn

Children and families

Children's counting games were common pastimes in the school yard, and many have been recorded by antiquarians. A common rhyme, thought to be derived originally from the Romany language of the travelling community and with many variants across the country, starts *"One-ery, two-ery"*; the particular Somerset version runs as follows:

One-ery, two-ery, hickary, hum,
Fillison, follison, Nicholson, John,
Quever, quauver, Irish Mary,
Stenkarum, stankarum, buck!

Children's rhyming couplets often feature local wildlife or folklore; one such is a warning against stealing eggs from robins' nests:

Who so robs the ruddick's nest,
Neither prospers nor is blest.

Children's nursery rhymes have travelled all over the country and even the globe, and it is rare that a particular location can lay claim to being the historical source of a rhyme. In Somerset, however, there is one such example. The rhyme goes:

Jack and Jill went up the hill
To fetch a pail of water.
Jack fell down and broke his crown,
And Jill came tumbling after.

The story goes that five hundred or so years ago, Jack and Jill were a pair of unmarried lovers who climbed to the well (which still exists today) at the top of Bad Stone Hill in the village of Kylmersdon. Jack fell and was killed by a boulder which broke free and rolled down the hill, crushing his skull and killing him instantly, while poor Jill died in childbirth a few days later. Roger Evans, a great champion of the Somerset dialect, notes that not only is Kylmersdon possessed of a well in an unconventional location at the top of a hill, but the rhyme only makes phonetic sense when recited in the Somerset dialect, so that *wadder* (water) rhymes with *adder* (after).

Punkie Night is a Somerset variant of Hallowe'en, occurring on the last Thursday in October every year and celebrated especially in south Somerset, particularly in the village of Hinton St George. A local story goes that the men of the village visited a fair in nearby Chiselborough and took all the lanterns with them. Once there they were so diverted by the young ladies at the fair (as well as a considerable amount of cider) that they stayed much longer than they had intended.

Thorpe village, 1909

Meanwhile, back at home, as night drew in their wives became concerned and wanted to organise a search for their menfolk. However, they had no lanterns, so they hollowed out mangel-wurzels or swedes and put candles inside them to make *punkies* (a dialect word for lantern, predating the use of pumpkins to make similar lights on Hallowe'en). With these light sources they set off in search of their errant husbands. In Chiselborough the men noticed the glowing lights approaching the village, and their state of inebriation (possibly combined with guilty consciences) caused them to mistake the lights for evil spirits. Seized by fear, they rushed for home by a long roundabout route to avoid the 'spirits' who appeared to be blocking their original route.

Of course, the women never let them forget their foolishness, and to this day the children of the village carry punkies on Punkie Night and sing the following song:

It's Punkie Night tonight,
It's Punkie Night tonight,
Adam and Eve would not believe
It's Punkie Night tonight!
Give me a candle, give me a light;
If you don't, you'll get a fright!

Church was an important part of country village life, with rectors and ministers often recording the customs and dialect of their parishioners in letters to friends and family elsewhere in the country, or indeed in scholarly publications on the subject. However, the fabric of church buildings and fittings is sometimes an unexpected source of dialect and the language (and sometimes the rivalries) of common folk. In the eighteenth century there seem to have been a number of rival bell-founders who may be called upon to cast and hang the bells for church steeples. They often cast inscriptions into their bells; most of these were sacred and serious in nature, but sometimes the founders took it upon themselves to record their own achievements and downplay those of their rivals.

One bell in Dunkerton church had the following inscription:

> *Before I was a broke I was as good as any;*
> *But when that Cokey casted I near was worth a penny.*

Backwell church contained a bell which proclaimed:

> *Bilby and Boosh may come and see*
> *What Evans and Nott have done by me.*

Fiddington village church, 1922

Finally, the tenor bell at Somerton church boasted:

> *Frind Wroth and Night, for all your Spite,*
> *Ould Edward Bilbie me rund.*
> *Pull me round and hear me sound*
> *Frind, such work you never do*

Somerset dialect contains proverbs aplenty; the following was recorded in the early nineteenth century by Miss Elizabeth Ham, a redoubtable Somerset spinster:

> *Bread an' cheese 'e' have a had,*
> *That 'e' had 'e' have eat,*
> *More 'e' would 'e' had it.*

(Meaning: I've eaten all the bread and cheese I had, but I would have eaten more if I'd had it.) As well as simple bread and cheese, there were many local delicacies in rural Somerset – not least the *wassail* (hot spiced apple punch or cider) which was served to revellers and offered to the orchards during the wassail ceremonies in January. Of course, Cheddar cheese deserves a special mention, named after the village of Cheddar and now ubiquitous in supermarkets across the country.

The *oggy* is a north Somerset version of the Cornish pasty, which is sometimes also known by the same name.

However, while Cornish oggies are D-shaped, with the crimped pastry crust running down the side of the pasty, the Somerset version has the crimped join across the mounded top, like the ridge of a roof. Both versions are often made with beef, but there is a specifically Somerset variant made with pork and Cheddar cheese.

Evening light looking down onto the village of Corton Denham
Shutterstock ©David Crosbie

Industry and agriculture

Apple cider production (and the wassailing which is a traditional part of the seasonal round) is such a profound part of Somerset history and culture that it comes as no surprise that there is an entire vocabulary devoted to this rural industry. Orchards were planted with standard trees to allow cattle and sheep to graze for most of the year, but when the apple harvest approached the beasts were removed and the orchards allowed to *hain* (grow in the absence of grazing stock). At harvest time the apples were collected from the ground and poled from the trees, avoiding the swarms of *apple drames* (wasps) who were attracted to the fallen fruit. After the main harvest a posse of small boys would assemble, go into the orchard with poles and bags and commence *griggling*, or knocking down the small apples (or *griggles*) left behind on the boughs.

The apples were collected in *maunds* (oval baskets) to be taken to the *pound* (or mill) to be *scratted* (chopped and crushed) to a *pomace* (a rough pulp). Traditionally the crushed apples were then laid down between layers of straw to form a *cheese*, which was placed in a *wring* (press) between boards to provide an even pressing. Finally weight or pressure was applied to extract the juice from the fruit. Then came the tricky business of fermentation, eventually producing the delicious *scrumpy* (cider) which made the whole laborious process worthwhile. It took a great quantity of apples to produce enough juice for a decent fermentation; it was generally accepted that it took twenty-one bushels of apples to produce a hogshead (a small barrel) of cider.

Small traditional cider presses are still available today – I have one of my own, made by a friend, powered by a bottle jack and fed by the labour of my children collecting and chopping apples from the six apple trees in our garden! An old rhyme captures the scene in the orchard, with the labourers hard at work and the farmer lending a hand in anticipation of the delicious cider to come:

All hans in archit busy be
A-polling apples off th' tree,
An' in th' wringhouse hard ta work
The mill da grine, the press da quirk;
The varmer, smilin' kine,
Da laff an joke an' help ez meyn
Ta mek th' Deb'nshir wine,
A-thinkin' when wi' pipe an' jug,
He'll zit in ez chim'ly carner snug.

Compton Dundon villagers outside the Castledrook Inn, c.1900

The Devonshire Redstreak was a very old variety of cider apple formerly grown in Somerset, although it may now be extinct; certainly few trees remained in the late eighteenth century, and it had become increasingly difficult to propagate from cuttings. *Devonshire wine* (cider made from Devonshire apples) was known as a superior concoction, sadly now lost to us.

Some areas of Somerset, particularly the uplands of the Mendips in northern Somerset, produce good quality quarried stone; indeed, Bath stone has been known and prized as an elegant building material for many centuries. However, the quarrymen who laboured to produce the stone were sometimes achingly poor, living in single-storey buildings which were barely considered to be dwellings at all: "*A house be'nt a home when he don't hev an up and a down.*"

One such worker, described in 1912 by the author H. Hay Wilson, was Nicholas Atwell, who lived with his wife Elizabeth in a tiny cabin tucked in a cleft in a hillside. Although Nicholas found work in the quarry near his home he was also known to be somewhat light-fingered, regularly taking what he needed from his friends and neighbours – but only from those who could afford to spare a little. This habit was rarely condemned by those who knew him; indeed, his victims often justified his actions and refused to press charges until the crimes became so blatant that they could be ignored no longer.

As one neighbour said after missing half a load of stone from his yard and simultaneously learning that Nicholas had sold a full load in the next town: "*I wouldn't persecute he for a matter o' a few score stones when 'tis like the rest of un was picked up here and picked up there, and did ought by rights to be restored to the Squire. Not but what rich folk hev a right to property, seein' 'tis theirn; but 'tis hard on the poor to go hungry when a load o' stones will fill un, in a manner o' speakin'.*"

In order to keep count of their sheep at a time when only the minority of people were numerate, shepherds all over the country used counting rhymes to take a tally of their flocks and make sure they hadn't lost any animals – as often happened, for they often made frantic bids for freedom through gates and holes in hedges:

They don't seem to know what do rightly want, let alone what be good for 'em. As if any witty beast, having got a good pasture, wouldn't be content and bide there.

The shepherd's counting rhymes are known generically as the *"yan, tan, tethera"* system, after the best-known variants in northern England, but West Country shepherds had their own system for counting to twenty as follows:

Hant, tant, tothery, fothery, fant, sahny, dahny, downy, dominy, dik, haindik, taindik, totherydik, fotherydik, jiggen, hain-jiggen, tain-jiggen, tother-jiggen, fother-jiggen, full-score.

When the full score of twenty animals was reached, a notch was made on a stick or tally post and the count would begin again.

Pig-keeping was a domestic matter, with each homestead usually raising its own animals for the table. However, pigs were notoriously likely to sicken and die – in fact, they were thought to be particularly susceptible to curses or the evil eye from ill-wishing neighbours. Being cantankerous beasts, it was also well known that they were usually resistant to veterinary attention; there was an old saying that *"there idn no drenchin a pig when he's a-took bad; there idn no cure vor'n but cold steel."*

Greenaleigh Farm, Minehead, 1920

Boats moored on the banks of the river Axe near Weston Super Mare
Shutterstock ©pphotoimages

Lack of education was never considered to be a hindrance among the farming community in Somerset. Indeed, sometimes it was thought of as an advantage. A young shepherd and prize sheep shearer was once laid up for weeks with a broken leg, and during that time he read through Treasure Island by Robert Louis Stevenson, sent in a goodwill parcel from the local Rectory to ease the invalid's suffering and hasten his recovery. On a visit to the farmhouse the parson was impressed by the boy's progress through the book, remarking to the lad's father that the boy was turning into a scholar. *"No, sure,"* replied the farmer, *"it don't stop in's head long enough to hurt 'en."*

A Dedication

The final word in this book should belong to James Jennings, a scholar and librarian of Queen's College, Cambridge in the mid-nineteenth century, but also a minister in Somerset and a faithful recorder of the local dialectical terms he heard among his flock. His writings have formed the source material for a good number of the terms in the earlier sections of this book, and the following is his own note to readers of his books, written in the dialect that he loved so much.

Thenk not, bin I ood be tha fashion
That I, Zir, write theaze Dedication;
I write, I haup I dwon't offend.
Bin I be proud ta call you Friend.
I here ston vooath, alooan unbidden
To 'muse you wi' my country lidden;
Wi' remlets o' tha Saxon tongue
That to our Gramfers did belong.
Vor all it is a little thing,
Receave it – friendship's offering -
Ta pruv, if pruf I need renew,
That I esteem not lightly You.

The Street, Wanstrow village, 1905

Bibliography

Many writers have celebrated and preserved the Somerset dialect, and as a consequence there is a wide variety of resources available. There is a broad range of modern material, written by enthusiastic and knowledgeable folk, but where possible I have tried to go as far back as possible to track down antiquarian sources who experienced the ancient dialect as it was spoken tens or even hundreds of years ago, or to attested literary works which record the local vernacular in the dialogue of the characters.

Among the most useful resources have been the following:

ELWORTHY, F.T., *On West Somerset patois*. Somerset Arch. and Nat. Hist. Soc. xxii. 31–46 (1876)

ELWORTHY, F.T., T*he West Somerset Word-Book of Dialectical and Archaic Words and Phrases used in the West of Somerset and East Devon* (English Dialect Society, 1886)

EVANS, R., *Don't Tell I, Tell 'Ee!* (Countryside Books, 2005)

JENNINGS, J., *The Dialect of the West of England Particularly Somersetshire* (Smith, 1825)

KNIGHT, F.A. & DUTTON, L.M.K., *Somerset* (Cambridge University Press, 1909)

WILLIAMS, W.P., *A Glossary of Provincial Words and Phrases in Use in Somersetshire* (Longmans, 1873)

WILSON, H.H., *A Somerset Sketch-Book* (Dent, 1912)

There is also a rich diversity of online resources, which have been collected and collated by many dedicated individuals.

Among the most interesting are:

THE BBC VOICES PROJECT:
http://www.bbc.co.uk/somerset/voices2005/

THE LOXTON VILLAGE HISTORICAL WEBSITE:
http://www.loxtonsomerset.org.uk/homepage.shtml

THE EXMOORIAN:
http://www.exmoorian.co.uk/dialect.htm

SOMERSET3D:
http://www.somerset3d.co.uk/speakinzummerzet.html